THE CHAVOUS/CHAVOUS-KAMBACH
CHRIST-FILLED RELATIONSHIP
EVALUATOR (C-FRE)

Understanding and Acting on Behaviors that lead to Christ-Filled Relationships

DR. ESTELLA CHAVOUS
with DR. JACINTA CK

©2025 Estella Chavous, Ed.D. The Doctoral Network. All rights reserved.

No part of this publication may be reproduced, stored in a retrieval system, or transmitted in any way by any means—electronic, mechanical, photocopy, recording, or otherwise—without the prior permission of the copyright holder, except as provided by USA copyright law. Contact: www.strategicladies.com.

Although the author and publisher have made every effort to ensure that the information in this book was correct at press time, the author and publisher do not assume and hereby disclaim any liability to any party for any loss, damage, or disruption caused by errors or omissions, whether such errors or omissions result from negligence, accident, or any other cause.

Unless otherwise noted all Scriptures taken from the Holy Bible, New International Version®, NIV®.

Copyright © 1973, 1978, 1984, 2011 by Biblica, Inc.™ Used by permission of Zondervan. All rights reserved worldwide. www.zondervan.com The "NIV" and "New International Version" are trademarks registered in the United States Patent and Trademark Office by Biblica, Inc.™

All Scripture quotations marked "KJV" are taken from the Holy Bible, King James Version, Cambridge, 1769.

Cover Design and Layout by
DocUmeant Designs
www.DocUmeantDesigns.com

ISBN: 9780692099407 19.95

Printed in the United States of America

CONTENTS

The Purpose of the C-FRE Evaluator and Booklet 1

Why Be Mind-FILLED? 2

Are Christians Christ-Filled? Why C-FRE Matters 2

    The Biblical Call to Grow 3

The C-FRE Evaluator 4

The Evaluator Assessment 5

Interpretation Results 6

    Your Overall Score: What It Means 7

    Your Individual Score: What It Means 8

    What's Next? 10

FILL Approach Explained
Christ-Filled Relationship Next Steps 10

    The Fill Approach 11

Closer Look at Awareness:
A Deep Dive into Awareness Results 15

    Awareness: The Foundation of Christ-Filled Living 15

    Tips on How to Improve Awareness with Christ 15

    Supporting Scriptures 16

    Journal & Devotional Reflection Topic—Awareness 16

Closer Look at Discernment:
A Deep Dive into Discernment results 19

    Tips on How to improve Discernment with Christ 19

    Supporting Scriptures 20

    Journal & Devotional Reflection Topic—Discernment 20

Closer Look at Emotion:
A Deep Dive into Emotion Results 23

    Supporting Scriptures 23

    Journal & Devotional Reflection Topic—Emotion 24

Closer Look at Renewal:
A Deeper Dive into Renewal Results 27
    Tips on How to experience a Renewal with Christ 27
    Supporting Scriptures 27
    Journal & Devotional Reflection Topic—Renewal 28

A Final Word 30

Christ-Filled Relationship Notes 31

References 35

The Purpose of the C-FRE Evaluator and Booklet

Purpose

The Chavous/Chavous-Kambach Christ-Filled Relationship Evaluator (C-FRE) is a practical, spiritually grounded tool designed to help individuals uncover their primary tendencies and growth areas in cultivating a Christ-Filled relationship. The assessment evaluates four foundational Christian behavioral categories:

- Awareness
- Discernment
- Emotion
- Renewal

Participants receive both an overall score and individual insights in each category. But C-FRE is more than a diagnostic tool—it is a call to action. It encourages Christians to grow personally and spiritually, equipping them to create change in their lives and in the lives of others. These results serve as a guide for spiritual accountability, lifelong learning, and the implementation of Christ-centered habits that strengthen individuals and teams alike.

This program is an invitation to deepen your walk with Christ. It offers practical insight and direction for building a meaningful and enduring Christ-Filled life, empowering believers with the knowledge and tools necessary to take charge of their spiritual journey.

Why Be Mind-Filled?

In Philippians 4:8–9, the apostle Paul writes:

"Finally, brethren, whatsoever things are true, whatsoever things are honest, whatsoever things are just, whatsoever things are pure, whatsoever things are lovely, whatsoever things are of good report—if there be any virtue, and if there be any praise—think on these things. What you have learned and received and heard and seen in me—practice these things, and the God of peace shall be with you."

Paul's words—**Learn, Take, Hear, Observe, and Do**—reveal what's often missing from secular mindfulness: intentional action rooted in God's Word.

To be *mind-filled* in a *Christ-filled* life means being present, not just with our thoughts, but with the truth and teachings of Jesus Christ. It involves actively incorporating biblical principles into our daily decisions, habits, and relationships.

Are Christians Christ-Filled? Why C-FRE Matters

The C-FRE booklet and assessment were created to help Christians actively **Learn, Take, Hear, Observe, and Do** God's Word. While many believers stand strong in their faith, we often struggle to navigate life's challenges. That struggle comes when we rely on our own strength—strength that is not enough to withstand the spiritual battles of this world.

But here's the **Good News: God's Word is enough**. His Word is living, powerful, and fully sufficient to fight our battles. Our responsibility is to fill ourselves with it and allow it to guide every part of our lives.

To support this idea, consider findings from a 2014 Gallup poll and a Huffington Post article that examined how American Christians view and use the Bible.

The Gallup poll, which surveyed over 1,000 adults, found that:

- 28% believe the Bible is the literal Word of God and should be taken word for word.
- 58% of Christians are more likely to affirm the Bible as the actual Word of God if allowed for multiple interpretations.

This reveals that while most Christians recognize the divine authority of Scripture, their views may vary on how literally it should be interpreted.

Even more striking are findings from the **Huffington Post (2013)**:

- 88% of Americans own a Bible.
- 80% believe the Bible is sacred.
- 61% wish they read it more.
- The average American household owns 4.4 Bibles.
- Yet, 57% read their Bibles four times a year or less.
- Only 26% read the Bible regularly (four or more times per week).

This is both encouraging and concerning. It's encouraging that the Bible holds a sacred place in many homes and hearts. But it's troubling that so few are actually reading it. Believing the Bible is God's Word is a powerful expression of faith—but faith must be followed by action. Too often, we rely on others to interpret or convey Scripture, rather than engaging with it ourselves.

As we enter an age that increasingly **edges God out**, it is essential that we intentionally work to **edge God in**—by embracing the Word, living by it, and building a personal relationship with Christ through it.

These studies affirm our belief in Scripture, but belief alone isn't enough. We must develop daily habits and Christ-centered behaviors that lead to transformation.

As 2 Timothy 2:15 reminds us:

"Study to show thyself approved unto God, a workman that needeth not to be ashamed, rightly dividing the word of truth."

God's Word was given to instruct, encourage, and guide us out of darkness and confusion. It reveals His desire for us and affirms that we are called to live holy lives—lives grounded in His purpose, grace, and truth through Jesus Christ.

A **Christ-Filled life** calls us to more than belief; it calls us to **obedience**. That means we must Learn, Take, Hear, Observe, and Do what is given to us in Scripture.

The **C-FRE program** helps guide this journey by focusing on four key Christ-Filled behavioral areas:

- Awareness
- Discernment
- Emotion
- Renewal

This booklet will help you begin the process of identifying your strengths and growth areas in each of these categories, preparing you for deeper reflection in Scripture and future steps in the program.

Let this be the beginning of your intentional walk toward a Christ-Filled life—grounded in the Word, led by the Spirit, and lived for God's glory.

The Biblical Call to Grow

2 Timothy 2:15 commands us:

"Study to show thyself approved unto God, a workman that needeth not to be ashamed, rightly dividing the word of truth."

The Bible was given for guidance, wisdom, and encouragement. It pulls us out of confusion and despair into truth, identity, and purpose. A Christ-Filled life calls us to act: to **Learn, Take, Hear, Observe, and Do.**

The **C-FRE program** equips us for this journey through four essential behaviors: Awareness, Discernment, Emotion, and Renewal. This booklet and assessment begin the process of identifying your strengths and growth areas in these categories, helping you step into a deeper walk with Christ and a clearer understanding of how to live out His Word.

The C-FRE Evaluator

If you haven't already completed the evaluator, this is your first step.

The **C-FRE Evaluator** provides a structured, biblical framework to help you reflect on your current behavioral patterns and how they align with a Christ-Filled life. It focuses on four essential categories:

- **Awareness** – Recognizing God's presence and your responses.
- **Discernment** – Making decisions rooted in biblical truth.
- **Emotion** – Understanding and managing God-given emotions.
- **Renewal** – Pursuing spiritual transformation and growth.

This assessment draws on scriptural principles to provide feedback on both individual and group tendencies. It's designed to uncover gaps and invite intentional spiritual alignment.

Directions:

- Read each pair of statements carefully.
- Choose the one that best represents your current behavior.
- There are no right or wrong answers—only honest reflection.
- If neither statement feels completely accurate, choose the one that's most like you.

Answer truthfully for the most meaningful results. Completing the evaluation should take only **3–5 minutes.**

Thank you for investing in your spiritual growth and helping to build the Kingdom of Christ—one heart and relationship at a time.

The Evaluator Assessment

Awareness

Discernment

Emotion

Renewal

Rate honestly the statement that is most characteristic of your behavior in the area of Awareness					
	Strongly Disagree	Disagree	Neutral	Agree	Strongly Agree
1. I fill my mind with God-centered material daily.	1	2	3	4	5
2. I recognize the source of self-focused and self-defeating thoughts.	1	2	3	4	5
3. The knowledge I have of the scriptures is through reading it myself.	1	2	3	4	5
4. I am content with my relationship with Christ.	1	2	3	4	5

Rate honestly the statement that is most characteristic of your behavior in the area of Emotion					
	Strongly Disagree	Disagree	Neutral	Agree	Strongly Agree
1. I find peace when I am in prayer and meditation.	1	2	3	4	5
2. I worry about nothing because all my needs will be supplied by Christ.	1	2	3	4	5
3. I use the power of God to control my emotions.	1	2	3	4	5
4. My emotions represent Christ's character.	1	2	3	4	5

Rate honestly the statement that is most characteristic of your behavior in the area of Discernment					
	Strongly Disagree	Disagree	Neutral	Agree	Strongly Agree
1. I have been given the gift of spiritual intuition.	1	2	3	4	5
2. I use the Bible to gain wisdom more than through life experiences.	1	2	3	4	5
3. I make judgments using God's word.	1	2	3	4	5
4. I am able to decide between truth and error, right and wrong.	1	2	3	4	5

Rate honestly the statement that is most characteristic of your behavior in the area of Renewal					
	Strongly Disagree	Disagree	Neutral	Agree	Strongly Agree
1. I take breaks to renew my mind with God's word throughout the day.	1	2	3	4	5
2. I am a good sleeper and can detach from my brain clutter.	1	2	3	4	5
3. I trust God in every situation.	1	2	3	4	5
4. I make regular changes to reflect a Godly lifestyle.	1	2	3	4	5

INTERPRETATION RESULTS

Scoring Your Evaluator Results

Congratulations! You've Taken the First Step Toward a Mind-FILLED Relationship with Christ.

Well done—you've completed the **Christ-Filled Relationship Evaluator (C-FRE)** and taken an intentional step toward deepening your relationship with Christ. Now, it's time to reflect on your results and explore what they reveal about your current walk with God.

Understanding the Evaluation

The **C-FRE** measures four foundational behaviors that reflect a Christ-filled life:

- Awareness
- Discernment
- Emotion
- Renewal

Rather than offering a simple "yes" or "no," the C-FRE uses a **Likert scale** to capture your level of agreement with each statement, allowing for nuanced insight into your thoughts, perceptions, and spiritual behaviors.

If you answered truthfully and thoughtfully, your results offer a meaningful and accurate picture of your spiritual positioning. Below we will look at both overall and individual behavior scoring.

Your Overall Score: What It Means

Overall Scoring Instructions

Each of your 16 responses is scored based on the following scale:

Strongly Agree—5

Agree—4

Neutral—3

Disagree—2

Strongly Disagree—1

Step 1: Add your total score from all 16 questions.

Step 2: Compare your total to the scoring ranges below:

- 1–26 ---→ Low Christ-Filled Relationship
- 27–54 ---→ Average Christ-Filled Relationship
- 55–80 ---→ High Christ-Filled Relationship

Step 3: Read the description that aligns with your score and reflect on your current Christ-Filled relationship findings.

High Christ-Filled Relationship (Score: 55–80)

Your results indicate that your life is deeply rooted in your relationship with Christ. You understand that a connection with God is not just important—it's foundational. You make God your first priority and recognize that all other relationships flow from that divine connection.

You actively apply biblical principles to real-life situations, drawing strength and direction from Scripture. God's Word is not just inspirational to you—it's essential, a daily source of wisdom, comfort, and clarity.

You also show a strong understanding that spiritual growth comes through a process: discernment becomes sharper, emotions align with truth, and personal renewal follows as you deepen your knowledge and connection with Christ.

You are walking in a fulfilling, Christ-filled life—and you're encouraged to keep learning, applying, and growing in Him.

As a result, spiritual discernment becomes clearer, your emotions are anchored in truth, and personal renewal follows. These behaviors naturally align through your relationship with Christ, leading to a **deeply fulfilling and joy-filled life**.

Keep pressing into God's presence, and let your life continue to reflect His Word.

Average Christ-Filled Relationship (Score: 27–54)

Your responses suggest that you have an **awareness of God's importance in your life,** but He may not yet be your daily focus. You believe the Bible is true and valuable, and you may even know how to apply it—but you may not be consistently using it to overcome life's challenges.

You might rely on sermons, devotionals, or others' interpretations of Scripture more than engaging with it personally. There may be a gap between what you believe and how often you practice it.

One or more of the four key behavior areas—**Awareness, Discernment, Emotion, or Renewal**—may need more intentional development. This is not a place of failure—it's a place of **opportunity**. God is inviting you to draw closer, to be mind-filled and heart-led by His truth.

Make a plan to deepen your habits and build more consistency with your spiritual walk. The growth you seek is within reach.

Low Christ-Filled Relationship (Score: 1–26)
Your responses reveal that your relationship with Christ may be **distant, undeveloped, or inconsistent**. It's possible that spiritual practices are reserved for special occasions or that your connection with Scripture feels unclear or unfamiliar.

You may not regularly apply biblical principles to daily challenges, and the Bible may not currently be a source of guidance in your life. This may be due to a lack of personal experience with God's Word, a new or emerging faith, or past spiritual disconnection.

But take heart—**this is not the end of the story**. The good news is that God is always ready to meet you where you are. Through intentional growth in the areas of **Awareness, Discernment, Emotion, and Renewal**, you can begin a transformative journey toward a Christ-Filled life.

This assessment is not a judgment—it's an invitation. God desires a personal, powerful relationship with you. He is ready when you are.

Your Individual Score: What It Means

Individual Scoring Instructions
Growth happens when we go deeper. Now, to do this, it's time to assess your individual **scores** across the four core Christ-filled behavior areas: Awareness, Discernment, Emotion, and Renewal. As with the overall score, each area was scored based on five targeted questions, using the same scoring system as before.

How to Score Your Individual Behavior Areas
Score Point Value

- **Strongly Agree**—5
- **Agree**—4
- **Neutral**—3
- **Disagree**—2
- **Strongly Disagree**—1

Step 1: Add your total score from the five questions in each category

Step 2: Locate your score range from the maximum of 20 points:

    1–6 ---→ Low Christ-Filled Relationship

    7–14 ---→ Average Christ-Filled Relationship

    15–20 ---→ High Christ-Filled Relationship

Step 3: Read the next page to discover what each score reveals about your Christ-filled behaviors—and how to grow in each area.

Each of the four core behavior areas—Awareness, Discernment, Emotion, and Renewal—reflects a vital component of a Christ-Filled relationship. Your individual scores in these areas provide insight into how consistently you embody Christ-centered behaviors in your daily life.

High Christ-Filled Relationship (Score: 15–20)

Your responses indicate a strong Christ-Filled relationship in this behavior area. You are actively engaging with God's Word, applying His truth, and reflecting His character in this aspect of your spiritual walk. Continue to deepen your growth by staying intentional and rooted in Christ.

Average Christ-Filled Relationship (Score: 7–14)

Your score shows that you are developing your Christ-Filled relationship in this area. You understand the importance of this behavior and may be applying it inconsistently. With more focus, intentional practice, and scriptural engagement, you can strengthen this area and align more closely with God's will.

Low Christ-Filled Relationship (Score: 1–6)

This score suggests that your Christ-Filled behaviors in this area are currently underdeveloped or rarely practiced. This is not a judgment—it's an opportunity. God is inviting you

ISBN 9781957832609 (pbk)
ISBN: 9781957832616 (ePub)
Available on-line and
at your local bookstore.

"Keep this Book of the Law always on your lips; meditate on it day and night, so that you may be careful to do everything written in it. Then you will be prosperous and successful" (Joshua 1:8).

to become more aware, discerning, emotionally aligned, or renewed through Him. With His help, growth is always possible.

What's Next?

Now that you have a clear picture of where you stand overall and in each individual behavior area, you're ready to take the next step.

FILL Approach Explained
Christ-Filled Relationship Next Steps

Many people ask, "Where do I begin?" The truth is we all learn differently. Just as we are diverse in personality and experience, we also vary in how we absorb and apply new knowledge. Adult learning can take many forms, including neuroscientific, experiential, self-directed, and transformational approaches. The key is not to focus on the method but on engagement.

As adult learners, we are most impacted when theory is combined with practical application. We seek understanding through real-world applications and appreciate opportunities to discover insights for ourselves.

Thankfully, the Bible was written with this in mind. The teachings of Christ are filled with real-life stories, lessons, and examples that help us apply godly wisdom in practical, everyday ways.

Jesus didn't just tell us what to do—He showed us. His life on Earth offers a clear and relatable model for how we are called to live.

If you begin your time in the Word with prayer and meditation, God will meet you there. He will reveal how you can align your life with His purpose and deepen your relationship with Christ.

How to begin your Christ-filled Learning Journey

Christ Map Branches

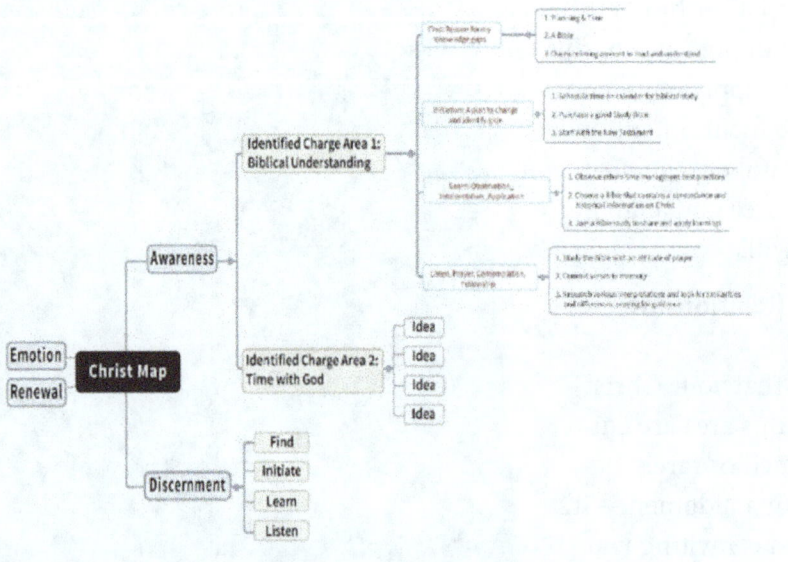

© 2025 www.strategicladies.com. All rights reserved

Two Keys to Starting a Christ-Filled Journey

As you begin or renew your walk with Christ, two powerful principles lay a strong foundation: preparedness and adopting an approach that truly FILLs your mind with God's Word.

Preparedness

A Christ-filled life doesn't happen by accident. It begins with intention—creating space in your heart, mind, and schedule to meet with God. Preparedness means setting aside time, gathering your spiritual tools (such as a Bible, journal, and prayer list), and opening your heart to what God wants to teach you. When you show up ready, God meets you there.

- Set intentional time aside for God daily—start with 10–15 minutes and build from there.
- Create a peaceful learning environment—somewhere you feel safe, focused, and comfortable.
- Prepare your tools—have your Bible, journal, concordance, dictionary, pen, paper, or computer handy.
- Talk to God intentionally—not just about what you want or need, but about what He wants you to know.
- Ask questions! Remember, God is your teacher. If you don't understand something, bring it to Him in prayer.

THE FILL APPROACH

The second key to a Christ-filled journey is embracing the FILL framework: Find, Initiate, Learn, Listen—a biblically grounded process designed to lead you into lasting spiritual transformation. It will help you understand what it truly means to fill your mind with Christ, as opposed to simply emptying it. This perspective is foundational to building a sustained, meaningful, and Spirit-led relationship with God.

Unlike secular practices that emphasize emptying the mind, the Christ-filled approach focuses on intentionally filling your mind with God's Word—truth, wisdom, and divine purpose. When our thoughts are aligned with His Word, our lives begin to reflect His will, creating space for genuine renewal and Christ-centered growth.

Let's explore each of these four steps and discover how they can help you live a more intentional, Spirit-led, Christ-centered life. To understand this approach, each step is explained below.

Step 1: FIND (Find your path to growth and Christ-centered change.)

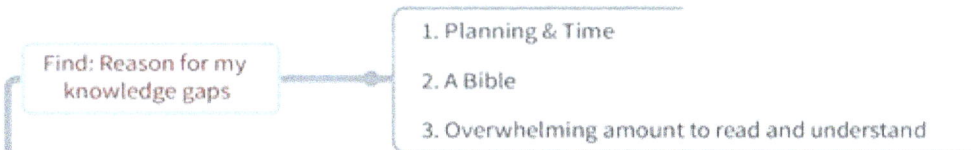

Start by establishing a clear, Spirit-led direction in your walk with God. What are your next steps? Do they include perseverance, prayer, and purpose? Use a journal to capture your thoughts, ideas, and commitments. Blank pages ae in this assessment booklet that you can use for this. Journaling helps quiet a wandering mind—a distraction often used by the enemy to pull us away from God's voice. Ensure this approach includes the steps you'll take, your desired Godly change, and the results you'd like to see.

The best example of the FIND approach is in a great story of change taught to us in the book of Ephesians, chapter 2. This story illustrates how God reconciled both Jews and Gentiles to Himself. In this book, the Apostle Paul shares a powerful testimony of transformation, urging us to "be made new in the attitude of your minds." This call to action unites all believers into one body, asking us to renew our thoughts, attitudes, and perspectives in line with God's will.

This verse sits within a larger framework:

- Ephesians 4:22 calls us to "*put off your old self,*" with its deceitful desires and corrupting influences.
- Ephesians 4:24 challenges us to "*put on the new self,*" created to be like God in true righteousness and holiness.

Together, these verses outline a transformative process rooted in Christ. It begins with being informed—choosing to reject ignorance and embrace truth. It continues with hearing and learning—actively receiving the Word of God. Then comes the shedding and renewing—letting go of old patterns and aligning with God's mindset. Finally, it culminates in wearing our Christ-centered identity—living out the righteousness and holiness we've received through Him. This is the path to true spiritual renewal and the ultimate example of divine transformation.

God calls us to seek Him intentionally. Finding His will for our lives begins with an openness to change and the courage to ask, "Lord, what would You have me do?" In Ephesians 4, Paul teaches us to "put off the old self" and walk in the newness of Christ. Finding your way is not about having it all figured out—it's about starting the journey with Him.

Step 2: INITIATE (Initiate personal change through a Christ Map.)

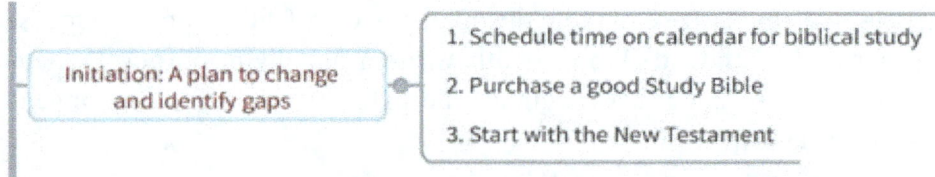

Your Personal Christ Map is a spiritual blueprint for transformation. Whether for individual growth or group development, it helps you identify what needs to change and guides you on how to start.

- Begin with a central topic (e.g., Emotional Renewal).
- Add branches of related behaviors or challenges.
- Add sub-branches with Scripture, prayers, or action steps.
- Choose one branch to focus on first.

Each branch could represent one of the mind-filled C-FRE Relationship Evaluator behaviors addressed in this survey, all of them or something quite different. Imagine the branches of a tree. Although separate, they connect to roots in the ground. These Christ Maps open many areas that call attention to in our Christ-filled lives.

God's Word is our roadmap. When you initiate change through His Word, you're guided by divine truth—not personal will. This approach mirrors the interconnectedness of a tree's roots and branches—different parts of your life, all grounded in God.

Faith is more than belief—it's action. Initiating change means stepping out in obedience, even when the outcome is unclear. God honors small beginnings (Zechariah 4:10). Like Peter stepping out of the boat, you don't need to walk on water—you just need to trust who you're walking toward. God has given us His roadmap to a Christ-filled life in His scriptures. We must be filled with the word to initiate it. Doing this will result in the spiritual relationship we desire and the relationship that He desires for us.

Step 3: LEARN (Learn and apply the truth of Scripture to every aspect of life.)

Real change starts with learning—and learning begins in God's Word. The Bible equips you with wisdom, correction, and encouragement for daily living.

2 Timothy 3:14–17 gives a good foundation for this: *"But continue thou in the things which thou hast learned and hast been assured of, knowing of whom thou hast learned them;* ¹⁵ *and that from a child thou hast known the holy scriptures, which can make thee wise unto salvation through faith which is in Christ Jesus.* ¹⁶ *All Scripture is given by inspiration of God, and is profitable for doctrine, for reproof, for correction, for instruction in righteousness:* ¹⁷ *that the man of God may be perfect, thoroughly furnished unto all good works"* (KJV).

From Genesis to Revelation, the Bible is a living, preserved document that remains unchanged in truth and power. It is the foundation for all Christ-filled living.

No book in the world has been copied and recopied as much as the Bible. Non-Christian scholars agree that the versions of the Bible we have today exhibit no substantial differences compared to the 1st-century manuscripts. God promised to preserve His written Word, and He has kept that promise throughout the centuries. In Luke 21:33, Jesus can say with complete confidence, *"Heaven and earth shall pass away, but my words shall not pass away."* It is for us to learn from the pure and the preserved.

2 Timothy 3:16 reminds us that all Scripture is God-breathed and useful for teaching, correction, and training in righteousness. Learning isn't just about knowledge—it's about letting the Word transform your mind and renew your heart. The more we read and reflect, the more we become like Christ.

Step 4: LISTEN

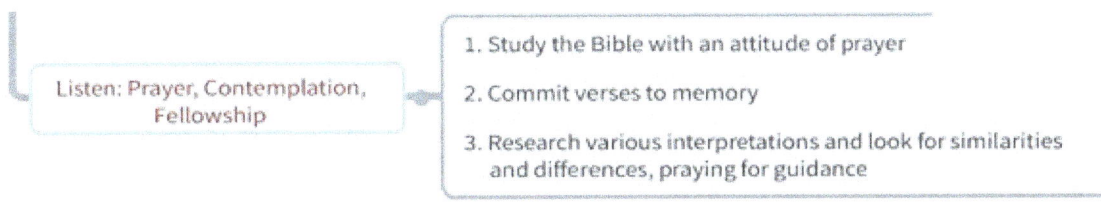

One of the best ways to listen to God is through prayer and biblical meditation. It is not surprising that prayer is understood, but meditation is not, given the current diverse meditation practices and their historical roots.

The best way to approach the practice of meditation, given to us by God, is to go to its source: the scripture. The type of meditation mentioned in the Bible does not ask us to empty our minds, but rather, it invites us to engage in biblical meditation. This engagement involves thoughtful consideration of His word and His teachings.

The Apostle Paul, in the 1st book of Timothy, wrote that pastors were taught how to conduct their lives and lead their churches. Because we learn from our pastors, whose role is to provide spiritual leadership to members, we, too, should follow the teachings of Paul.

Understanding prayer is important, but we should do this by not overlooking the value of biblical meditation.

1 Timothy 4:15–16 tells us to *"Meditate upon these things; give thyself wholly to them; that thy profiting may appear to all."* Paul encouraged leaders to meditate on God's truth and live it out so that their growth would be visible and transformational.

You do this by listening, which requires stillness. Christian meditation differs from secular meditation in that it teaches us to fill our minds with God's Word and allow it to dwell richly within us.

In the noise of life, God speaks not always in the thunder but in the whisper (1 Kings 19:12). Colossians 3:16 reminds us: *"Let the word of Christ dwell in you richly."*

That's what biblical meditation does—it invites God's truth to take residence in your heart and direct your steps.

Start with 5 minutes of scripture reading followed by 5 minutes of reflection. Ask the Holy Spirit through prayer to respond and illuminate what God wants you to hear and how He wants you to respond. Through prayer and biblical meditation, we tune our hearts to His voice. Listening to God brings wisdom, peace, and direction.

The C-FRE Evaluator has helped you identify your current standing in your Christ-filled relationship—both overall and in each behavioral category. Acting on this takes preparedness and approaches like FILL to deepen your Christ-filled relationship and sustain lasting change. It is now time to head to the "A Closer Look" section for each behavior area. There, you'll begin your dive deeper into Christ-filled activities that support growth and transformation.

Closer Look at Awareness: A Deep Dive into Awareness Results

Awareness: The Foundation of Christ-Filled Living

This section explores **Awareness** and how it shapes your relationship with Christ. As you reflect on your individual score, consider how much this area needs growth in your own life—and how you might support others in developing it as well.

But first, what exactly is awareness?

According to Merriam-Webster, **awareness** is *"the ability to directly know, perceive, feel, or be conscious of something."* In spiritual terms, awareness means being consciously attuned to God's presence—recognizing His hand in your everyday life and being sensitive to His voice, His Word, and His will.

Awareness is a critical catalyst for change. Without it, we become spiritually stagnant. In fact, a lack of awareness is one of the biggest obstacles to forming a meaningful relationship with Christ. To overcome this, we must begin by paying attention—truly observing how God is integrated into our thoughts, emotions, relationships, and daily experiences.

This includes:

- Becoming more self-aware of how your actions align with His will.
- Observing how God shows up in the small and large moments of life.
- Noticing when your focus has shifted away from Him—and intentionally bringing it back.

Take time to get to know yourself and how God is working in you. Consider how you can use your awareness to grow your faith and help others recognize God's presence in their own lives. Use the journal worksheet and the insights here to identify areas where you can FILL in the gaps and move toward a stronger, more Christ-Filled relationship.

Tips on How to Improve Awareness with Christ

- Be mindful of how you spend time with God.
- Schedule intentional time for prayer, reflection, and worship.
- Read Scripture with purpose—set daily goals to learn something new.
- Examine the roots of self-defeating thoughts and replace them with biblical truth.
- Live a life of obedience and surrender to Christ.
- Be **mind-FILLED** with God's truth rather than mind-FULL of distractions.

Supporting Scriptures

Matthew 6:26 *"Look at the birds of the air, for they neither sow nor reap nor gather into barns; yet your heavenly Father feeds them. Are you not of more value than they?"*

→ God's care is constant—when we are aware of His provision, fear and anxiety diminish.

1 Corinthians 9:24–25 *"In this life, we can run the race so as to win an imperishable crown in the next. We cannot do this through our own effort."*

→ Stay spiritually alert—awareness drives us to run our race with purpose.

Ephesians 6:12 *"For we wrestle not against flesh and blood, but against principalities, against powers, against the rulers of the darkness of this world, against spiritual wickedness in high places."*

→ Awareness reminds us of the unseen spiritual battles and the power we have in Christ.

Joshua 1:8 *"This book of the law shall not depart out of thy mouth; but thou shalt meditate therein day and night, that thou may observe to do according to all that is written therein: for then thou shalt make thy way prosperous, and then thou shalt have good success."*

→Constant reflection on God's Word awakens spiritual awareness and leads to fruitful living.

Journal & Devotional Reflection Topic—Awareness

Step 1: Select your Score ranking (High—Medium—Low)

High Christ-Filled Relationship
If you scored 15–20, your behaviors indicate that you have a high level of Christ-Filled relationship in Awareness.

Devotional Reflection/ Prayer:(Meditate on this)

I have built my foundation on Christ, and it shows in my daily actions, thoughts, and spiritual discipline. But the journey of faith is not about arriving—it's about abiding. Thank you, God, for calling me to go deeper and strengthen my inner life.

—Psalm 127:1 (NIV.) tells us that, *"Unless the Lord builds the house, the builders labor in vain."* Thank you, God, for the stillness; as it is in that stillness, you speak to me and lead me in the direction you would have me go.

Average Christ-Filled Relationship
If you scored 7–14, your behaviors indicate that you have an average Christ-Filled relationship in Awareness.

Devotional Reflection/Prayer: (Meditate on this)

I meet with God daily and believe in His Word. I have learned that between belief and practice, it is His Holy Spirit that gives me more consistency, more intimacy, and more power. *"Draw near to God, and He will draw near to you"* —James 4:8 (ESV).

Thank you for the discipline I have in carving out time for you, giving me a heart to want more.

Low Christ-Filled Relationship
If you scored 1–6, your behaviors indicate that you have a low Christ-Filled relationship in Awareness.

Devotional Reflection/Prayer: (Meditate on this)

I am not unsure about my relationship with God, as I have begun to grow in faith because I now know that he is simply waiting for me to come.

"Come to me, all who are weary and burdened, and I will give you rest"—Matthew 11:28 (NIV).

Thank you, Jesus, for offering me a relationship with you and for providing answers to my questions through Your Word. I know that I am not worthy to receive you but only say the word and I am healed.

Step 2: Take your score and apply FILL (Find—Initiate—Listen—Learn)

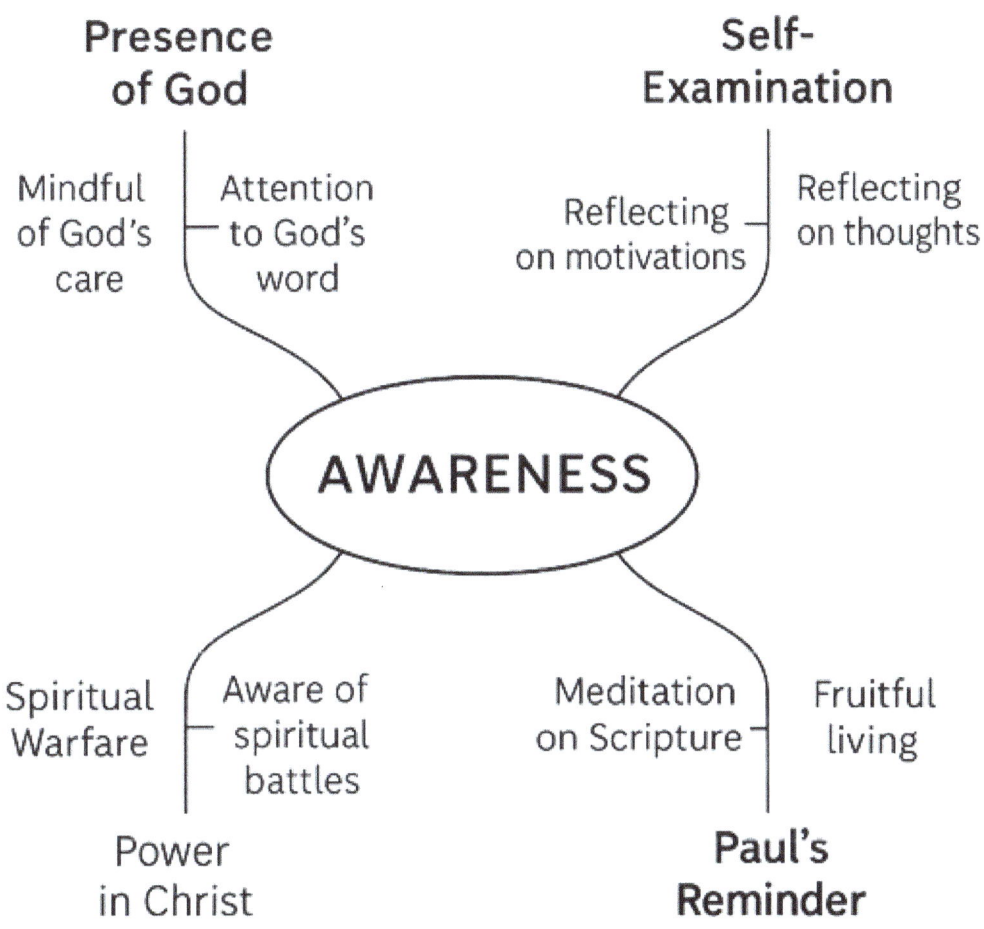

Find: Find your behavioral change. Journal the desired change you'd like to see in biblical awareness. Include how you plan to initiate this change and outline the goals for the desired outcome. How did you score in this area, and what behaviors are driving your score?

Initiate: Start with a Christ Map—This is a documented plan for implementing your change. Write down the steps, how you are going to implement the steps, and the information needed for success. Does your Christ Map contains a plan that includes learning, hearing, observing, and doing.

Learn: Learn God's word. It communicates from Genesis to Revelation that God is intimately involved in, familiar with, and concerned for us. All truths are found in the scripture for any of our needs. What have you learned from God's word in theory and practice?

Listen: Prayer and meditation are the best ways to hear God. Consider the benefits of listening to the change God has for us versus what we see for ourselves. How have prayer and meditation helped you develop a more personal relationship with Christ?

_____
_____
_____
_____
_____
_____
_____
_____
_____
_____
_____
_____
_____
_____
_____
_____
_____
_____

Closer Look at Discernment:
A Deep Dive into Discernment results

This section focuses on **Discernment** and how this behavior shapes your walk with Christ. As you reflect on your score, consider how much you may need to grow in this area—or how you might support others in strengthening it.

To begin, we must understand what **discernment** truly is.

Discernment is the ability to judge well. In Christian life, it goes deeper—it is the Spirit-led capacity to perceive God's will, distinguish truth from deception, and understand the difference between right and wrong. It is the act of seeking spiritual insight with humility and faith, not just through intellect, but through prayerful wisdom and study of the Word (Merriam-Webster Dictionary, n.d.).

Biblically, discernment is vital. It empowers us to live wisely, avoid spiritual pitfalls, and stand firm in truth—especially in a world filled with distractions and false teachings. Without discernment, believers risk drifting into complacency or compromise. But with it, we build lives of accountability, integrity, and sound doctrine.

This area can be especially challenging if we don't regularly engage with God's Word ourselves. A Christ-Filled life must be rooted in the Bible—lived out through obedience, not opinion. The goal is not perfection, but alignment with God's truth.

Take time to reflect:

- How do you respond when faced with spiritual confusion or moral dilemmas?
- Are your decisions shaped by Scripture, or by popular opinion?
- How can you grow in spiritual maturity and help others do the same?

Discernment is not just for the individual—it has a powerful ripple effect. Use it to lead teams, serve communities, and guide others toward a clearer understanding of Christ.

Use the insights on this page to identify areas for growth, fill any gaps, and inspire others toward a more Christ-Filled relationship and journal in the blank pages in the end of this booklet.

Tips on How to improve Discernment with Christ

- Judge not hypocritically
- Know your spiritual gifts
- Use scripture for ethical and moral direction
- Gain knowledge through the study of God's word
- Seek God's opinion, not man's
- Live for heavenly versus earthly things

SUPPORTING SCRIPTURES

Matthew 7:1–2 *"Judge not, that you be not judged. For with what judgment you judge, you will be judged; and with the measure you use, it will be measured back to you."*

1 Corinthians 12:4 *"There are different kinds of gifts, but the same Spirit distributes them."*

Psalm 37:30 *"The mouths of the righteous utter wisdom, and their tongues speak what is just."*

Proverbs 2:6 *"For the LORD gives wisdom; from his mouth come knowledge and understanding."*

Galatians 1:10 *"For do I persuade men or God? Or do I seek to please men? For if I please men, I should not be the servant of Christ."*

Colossians 3:2 *"Set your affection on things above, not on earthly things."*

JOURNAL & DEVOTIONAL REFLECTION TOPIC—DISCERNMENT

Step 1: Select your Score ranking (High—Medium—Low)

High Christ-Filled Relationship
If you scored 15–20, your behaviors indicate that you have a high level of Christ-Filled relationship in Discernment.

Devotional Reflection/Prayer:(Meditate on this)

I have built my foundation on Christ, and it shows in my daily actions, thoughts, and spiritual discipline. But the journey of faith is not about arriving—it's about abiding. Thank you, God, for calling me to go deeper and strengthen my inner life.

—Psalm 127:1 (NIV.) tells us that, *"Unless the Lord builds the house, the builders labor in vain."* Thank you, God, for the stillness; as it is in that stillness, you speak to me and lead me in the direction you would have me go.

Average Christ-Filled Relationship
If you scored 7–14, your behaviors indicate that you have an average Christ-Filled relationship in Discernment.

Devotional Reflection/Prayer: (Meditate on this)

I meet with God daily and believe in His Word. I have learned that between belief and practice, it is His Holy Spirit that gives me more consistency, more intimacy, and more power. *"Draw near to God, and He will draw near to you"* —James 4:8 (ESV).

Thank you for the discipline I have in carving out time for you, giving me a heart to want more.

Low Christ-Filled Relationship
If you scored 1–6, your behaviors indicate that you have a low Christ-Filled relationship in Discernment.

Devotional Reflection/Prayer: (Meditate on this)

I am not unsure about my relationship with God, as I have begun to grow in faith because I now know that he is simply waiting for me to come.

"Come to me, all who are weary and burdened, and I will give you rest"—Matthew 11:28 (NIV).

Thank you, Jesus, for offering me a relationship with you and for providing answers to my questions through Your Word. I know that I am not worthy to receive you but only say the word and I am healed.

Step 2: Take your score and apply FILL (Find—Initiate—Listen—Learn)

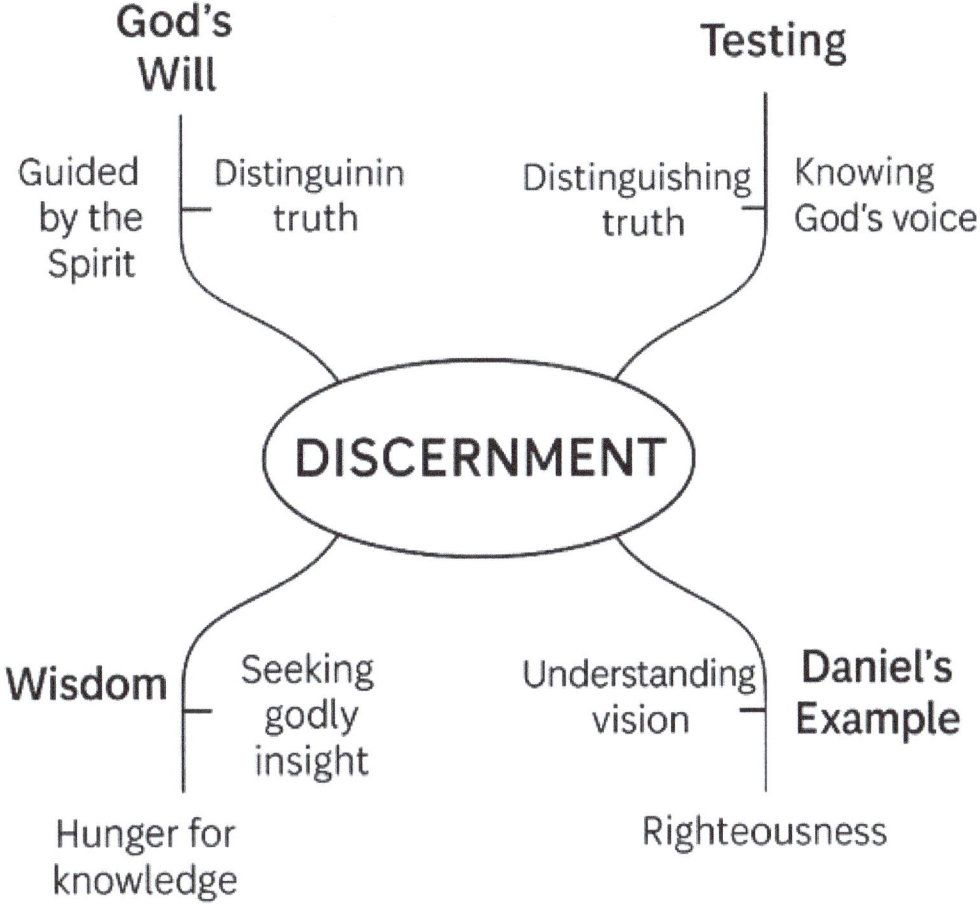

- Find your Behavioral Change Area
- Initiate a Christ Map
- Learn God's Word
- Listen to God using Prayer and Meditation

Find: Find: Find your behavioral change. Journal the desired change you'd like to see in biblical discernment. Include how you are going to start this change and what the goals are for the outcome. How did you score in this area, and what behaviors are driving your score?

Initiate: Start with a Christ Map—This is a documented plan for implementing your change. Write down the steps, how you are going to implement the steps, and the information needed for success. Does your Christ Map contains a plan that includes learning, hearing, observing, and doing.

Learn: Learn God's word. It communicates from Genesis to Revelation that God is intimately involved in, familiar with, and concerned for us. All truths are found in the scripture for any of our needs. What have you learned from God's word in theory and practice?

Listen: Prayer and meditation are the best ways to hear God. Consider the benefits of listening to the change God has for us versus what we see for ourselves. How have prayer and meditation helped you develop a more personal relationship with Christ?

_____
_____
_____
_____
_____
_____
_____
_____
_____
_____
_____
_____
_____
_____
_____

Closer Look at Emotion: A Deep Dive into Emotion Results

This section focuses on on emotions and how they affect your walk with Christ. As you review your score, gauge the extent to which you need to develop or support others in this area. To do this, we must first understand what emotion is.

Emotion is a natural, instinctive state of mind deriving from one's circumstances, mood, or relationships with others.

It is also an instinctive or intuitive feeling as distinguished from reasoning or knowledge (Merriam-Webster Dictionary, n.d.). Emotions come with great intensity and are a struggle to manage for most of us. They also authenticate our understanding of the truth that can be found in God's word. We should learn to manage our emotions through the strong principles laid out for us in the Bible. We are created in God's image, and His emotions and how He would like us to display them are revealed in the scriptures.

Take time to get to know yourself, identifying ways you can maximize your emotional well-being and help support this area in others. Consider how you can utilize emotions to gain insight into groups and teams, thereby bringing others closer to the knowledge of Christ. Use the Journal worksheet and the information on this page to fill any gaps and motivate others toward a Christ-filled relationship.

Tips on How to improve Emotions with Christ

- Be mindful of your words
- Follow the direction of God
- Know that God cares for you
- God will fulfill all of your needs
- In the Spirit of the Lord, you will find peace
- God is always there to comfort you

Supporting Scriptures

Exodus 4:12 *"Now then go, and even I will be with your mouth, and teach you what you are to say."*

2 Peter 1:21 *"For no prophecy was ever made by an act of human will, but men moved by the Holy Spirit spoke from God."*

Psalm 55:22 *"Cast your cares on the Lord and he will take care of you. He will not permit the godly to slip and fall."*

Ephesians 3:19 *"And to know the love of Christ which surpasses knowledge, that you may be filled up to all the fullness of God."*

Romans 12:18 *"Be Diligent to preserve the unity of the spirit in the bond of peace."*

Psalm 23:4 *"Even though I walk through the darkest valley, I will fear no evil, for you are with me, your rod and your staff, they comfort me."*

Additional Scriptures

Matthew 6:33–34 *"But seek first the kingdom of God and His righteousness, and all of these things will be added to you. Therefore, do not worry about tomorrow, for tomorrow will worry about itself. Each day has its own trouble."*

Philippians 4:6–7 *"Do not be anxious about anything, but in everything, by prayer and petition, with thanksgiving, present your requests to God. And the peace of God, which transcends all understanding, will guard your hearts and minds in Christ Jesus."*

James 1:19–20 *"My beloved brothers, everyone should be quick to listen, slow to speak, and slow to wrath. For the wrath of man does not produce the righteousness of God."*

1 John 4:7 *"Beloved, let us love one another, because love is from God."*

Colossians 3:12 *"Therefore, as the chosen ones of God, holy and beloved, put on compassion, mercy, benevolence, humility, gentleness, and patience.*

JOURNAL & DEVOTIONAL REFLECTION TOPIC—EMOTION

Step 1: Select your Score ranking (High—Medium—Low)

High Christ-Filled Relationship
If you scored 15–20, your behaviors indicate that you have a high Christ-Filled relationship in Emotion.

Devotional Reflection/ Prayer:(Meditate on this)

I have built my foundation on Christ, and it shows in my daily actions, thoughts, and spiritual discipline. But the journey of faith is not about arriving—it's about abiding. Thank you, God, for calling me to go deeper and strengthen my inner life.

—Psalm 127:1 (NIV.) tells us that, *"Unless the Lord builds the house, the builders labor in vain."* Thank you, God, for the stillness; as it is in that stillness, you speak to me and lead me in the direction you would have me go.

Average Christ-Filled Relationship
If you scored 7–14, your behaviors indicate that you have an average Christ-Filled relationship in Emotion.

Devotional Reflection/Prayer: (Meditate on this)

I meet with God daily and believe in His Word. I have learned that between belief and practice, it is His Holy Spirit that gives me more consistency, more intimacy, and more power. *"Draw near to God, and He will draw near to you."* —James 4:8 (ESV)

Thank you for the discipline I have in carving out time for you, giving me a heart to want more.

Low Christ-Filled Relationship
If you scored 1–6, your behaviors indicate that you have a low Christ-Filled relationship in Emotion.

Devotional Reflection/Prayer: (Meditate on this)

I am not unsure about my relationship with God, as I have begun to grow in faith because I now know that he is simply waiting for me to come.

"Come to me, all who are weary and burdened, and I will give you rest"—Matthew 11:28 (NIV).

Thank you, Jesus, for offering me a relationship with you and for providing answers to my questions through Your Word. I know that I am not worthy to receive you but only say the word and I am healed.

Step 2: Take your score and apply FILL (Find—Initiate—Listen—Learn)

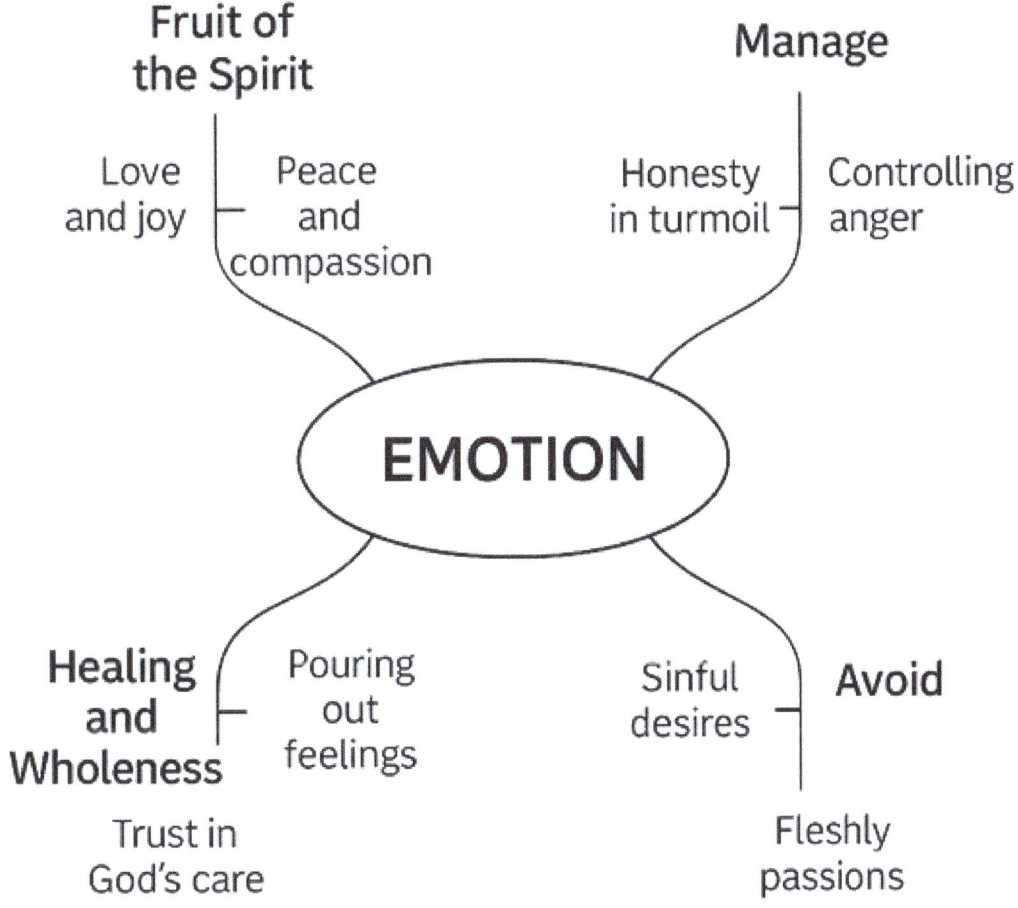

- Find your Behavioral Change Area
- Initiate your Christ Map
- Learn God's Word
- Listen to God using Prayer and Meditation

Find: Find: Find your behavioral change. Journal the desired change you'd like to see in biblical emotion. Include how you are going to start this change and what the goals are for the outcome. How did you score in this area, and what behaviors are driving your score?

Initiate: Start with a Christ Map—This is a documented plan for implementing your change. Write down the steps, how you are going to implement the steps, and the information needed for success. Does your Christ Map contains a plan that includes learning, hearing, observing, and doing.

Learn: Learn God's word. It communicates from Genesis to Revelation that God is intimately involved in, familiar with, and concerned for us. All truths are found in the scripture for any of our needs. What have you learned from God's word in theory and practice?

Listen: Prayer and meditation are the best ways to hear God. Consider the benefits of listening to the change God has for us versus what we see for ourselves. How have prayer and meditation helped you develop a more personal relationship with Christ?

_____
_____
_____
_____
_____
_____
_____
_____
_____
_____
_____
_____
_____

Closer Look at Renewal: A Deeper Dive into Renewal Results

This section focuses on renewal and how this behavior affects your walk with Christ. As you review your score, gauge the extent to which you need to develop or support others in this area.

To do this, we must first understand what Renewal is. Renewal is the process of replacing something that is worn out, run-down, or broken.

Among charismatic Christians, it is the state or process of being made spiritually new in the Holy Spirit (Merriam-Webster Dictionary, n.d.). The focus on Renewal and new life with God should not just be left to being born again or your first acceptance of Christ. We must work to make a fresh start in our daily walk with God.

Making changes to our lives can be difficult, so instead of focusing on how we can improve ourselves, consider how God is working to improve us as we continue to read and stay in His word. That is when the renewal process becomes sustainable and a natural form of change. Take time to get to know yourself, identifying ways you can maximize your Renewal and help support this area in others.

Consider how you can renew your relationship with God and gain insight into supporting groups and teams. Use the Journal worksheet and the information on this page to fill any gaps and motivate others toward a Christ-filled relationship.

Tips on How to experience a Renewal with Christ

- Work to have the mental attitude of Christ
- Trust in all that God gives you
- Cease striving, and know that he is God
- God renews you moment to moment
- Take time for Christ breaks and Christ-FILLED renewals
- *God is your problem solver*

Supporting Scriptures

Matthew 6:26 *"Look at the birds of the air, for they neither sow nor reap nor gather into barns; yet your heavenly Father feeds them. Are you not of more value than they?"*

1 Corinthians 2:16 *"For he hast known the mind of the lord, that he may instruct him? But we have the mind of Christ."*

Psalms 46:10 *"Be Still, and know that I am God: I will be exalted among the heathen; I will be exalted in the earth."*

Isaiah 43:18–19 *"Remember ye not the former things, neither consider the things of old, Behold I will do a new thing; now it shall spring forth; shall you not know it? I will even make a way in the wilderness, and rivers in the desert."*

1 Peter 5:7 *"Casting all your cares upon him, for he careth for you."*

Additional Scripture

Romans 12:2 *"Be no longer conformed to this world, but be transformed by the renewing of your mind, so that you might be able to test and approve God's will, his good, pleasing, and perfect will."*

Journal & Devotional Reflection Topic—Renewal

Step 1: Select your Score ranking (High—Medium—Low)

High Christ-Filled Relationship
If you scored 15–20, your behaviors indicate that you have a high Christ-Filled relationship in Renewal.

Devotional Reflection/ Prayer:(Meditate on this)

I have built my foundation on Christ, and it shows in my daily actions, thoughts, and spiritual discipline. But the journey of faith is not about arriving—it's about abiding. Thank you, God, for calling me to go deeper and strengthen my inner life.

—Psalm 127:1 (NIV.) tells us that, *"Unless the Lord builds the house, the builders labor in vain."* Thank you, God, for the stillness; as it is in that stillness, you speak to me and lead me in the direction you would have me go.

Average Christ-Filled Relationship
If you scored 7–14, your behaviors indicate that you have an average Christ-Filled relationship in Renewal.

Devotional Reflection/Prayer: (Meditate on this)

I meet with God daily and believe in His Word. I have learned that between belief and practice, it is His Holy Spirit that gives me more consistency, more intimacy, and more power. *"Draw near to God, and He will draw near to you"* —James 4:8 (ESV).

Thank you for the discipline I have in carving out time for you, giving me a heart to want more.

Low Christ-Filled Relationship
If you scored 1–6, your behaviors indicate that you have a low Christ-Filled relationship in Renewal.

Devotional Reflection/Prayer: (Meditate on this)

I am not unsure about my relationship with God, as I have begun to grow in faith because I now know that he is simply waiting for me to come.

"Come to me, all who are weary and burdened, and I will give you rest"—Matthew 11:28 (NIV).

Thank you, Jesus, for offering me a relationship with you and for providing answers to my questions through Your Word. I know that I am not worthy to receive you but only say the word and I am healed.

Step 2: Take your score and apply FILL (Find—Initiate—Listen—Learn)

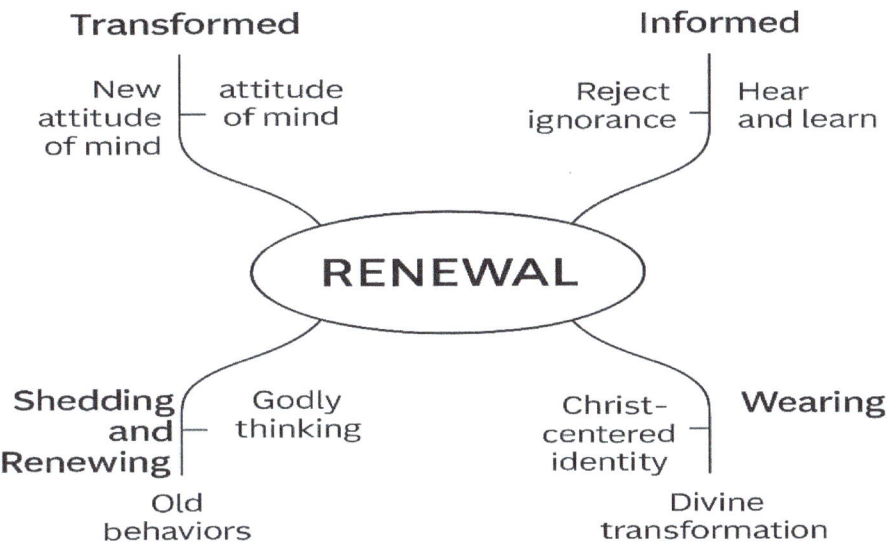

- Find your Behavioral Change Area
- Initiate a Christ Map
- Learn God's Word
- Listen to God using Prayer and Meditation

Find: Find your behavioral change. Journal the desired change you'd like to see in biblical Renewal. Include how you are going to start this change and what the goals are for the outcome. How did you score in this area, and what behaviors are driving your score?

Initiate: Start with a Christ Map—This is a documented plan for implementing your change. Write down the steps, how you are going to implement the steps, and the information needed for success. Does your Christ Map contains a plan that includes learning, hearing, observing, and doing.

Learn: Learn God's word. It communicates from Genesis to Revelation that God is intimately involved in, familiar with, and concerned for us. All truths are found in the scripture for any of our needs. What have you learned from God's word in theory and practice?

Listen: Prayer and meditation are the best ways to hear God. Consider the benefits of listening to the change God has for us versus what we see for ourselves. How have prayer and meditation helped you develop a more personal relationship with Christ?

_____

_____

_____

A Final Word

The practical advice and fundamental behaviors outlined in this booklet can empower you to improve various aspects of your Christian life, moving you towards a more Christ-centered existence. As you navigate through work and play, revisit this booklet to see how you can enhance or develop in any of these behaviors. Living a sustained Christ-filled life requires effort and a commitment to staying in the scripture. Being Christ-filled empowers you to work through issues you face in conflict, accountability, emotional intelligence, and the perception you've created for yourself and others.

For more information on Christ-Filled Courses, Workshops, Christ Maps, and Interactive Activities related to the C-FRE evaluator, email me at: office@stategicladies.com.

Christ-Filled Relationship Notes

Christ-Filled Relationship Notes

Christ-Filled Relationship Notes

REFERENCES

Awareness. (n.d.). In Merriam-Webster's Online Dictionary. Retrieved from https://www.merriam-webster.com/dictionary/awareness

Bell, C. (2013). *Americans Love the Bible but Don't Read It Much, Poll Shows.* Retrieved from https://www.huffingtonpost.com/2013/04/04/americans-love-the-bible-but-dont-read-it-much_n_3018425.html

Bible online, KJV, NIV, & Geneva Versions

Discernment. (n.d.). In Merriam-Webster's Online Dictionary. Retrieved from https://www.merriam-webster.com/dictionary/discernment

Emotion. (n.d.). In Merriam-Webster's Online Dictionary. Retrieved from https://www.merriam-webster.com/dictionary/emotion

Renewal. (n.d.). In Merriam-Webster's Online Dictionary. Retrieved from https://www.merriam-webster.com/dictionary/renewal

The Two Way Breaking News. (n.d.). *Most Americans See Bible as Word of God, Gallup*

Says, 2014. Retrieved from https://www.npr.org/sections/thetwo-way/.

www.ingramcontent.com/pod-product-compliance
Lightning Source LLC
Chambersburg PA
CBHW082248300426
44110CB00039B/2482